BRIDAL FASHION
1900–1950

Kathleen York

SHIRE PUBLICATIONS

Published in Great Britain in 2012 by Shire Publications
Ltd, Midland House, West Way, Botley, Oxford OX2 0PH,
United Kingdom.

44-02 23rd Street, Suite 219, Long Island City, NY 11101,
USA.

E-mail: shire@shirebooks.co.uk   www.shirebooks.co.uk

Every attempt has been made by the Publishers to secure
the appropriate permissions for materials reproduced in
this book. If there has been any oversight we will be happy
to rectify the situation and a written submission should be
made to the Publishers.

A CIP catalogue record for this book is available from the
British Library.

Shire Library no. 706.   ISBN-13: 978 0 74781 200 5

Kathleen York has asserted her right under the Copyright,
Designs and Patents Act, 1988, to be identified as the
author of this book.

Designed by Tony Truscott Designs, Sussex, UK
and typeset in Perpetua and Gill Sans.

Printed in China through Worldprint Ltd.

12 13 14 15 16   10 9 8 7 6 5 4 3 2 1

COVER IMAGE
Actress Gene Tierney in the film version of W. Somerset
Maugham's *The Razor's Edge* wears an ensemble not atypical
of the wealthy brides of the early twentieth century.

TITLE PAGE IMAGE
This bride and her bridesmaids are wearing Hollywood-
inspired headpieces of satin and velvet over wire frames.

CONTENTS PAGE IMAGE
From Harvey, Illinois, this bride and her bridesmaids are
all wearing different dresses, which are fine examples of
the styles that were popular in the 1920s.

ACKNOWLEDGEMENTS
I wish to thank my family for the use of our family bridal
pictures in this book.

PHOTO CREDITS
I would like to thank the people who have allowed me to
use bridal pictures, which are noted as follows: Kenneth
Kikel, Linda Fowler, and James Kikel: pages 13 and 40
(upper left); Barbara Kikel: page 36; Ruth and Robert
Fischer: page 42. All other photographs are from the
author's collection.

Shire Publications is supporting the Woodland Trust, the UK's leading woodland conservation charity, by funding the dedication of trees.

CONTENTS

INTRODUCTION

For millennia, weddings have been important events, marking milestones in the lives of couples as they embark on new lives together. Weddings have changed greatly over the years, from simple, religious affairs with a few family members to dazzling galas for hundreds of guests for which some couples spend tens of thousands of dollars.

Weddings are big business. One of the most expensive and most critiqued items of the wedding day is the bride's gown.

Here in the early 2010s, bridal fashions are a separate genre and do not reflect the way the average woman dresses. Today, brides want to look like a "princess" or "sexy siren" in dress styles called "ball gown" with a full skirt, or "mermaid" with a body-hugging top and flared skirt starting at the knees.

This was not always the way. In the past, bridal fashions reflected the style of dress worn daily. While today, many brides favor elaborate gowns with beading, lace, and "bling," dresses of the early twentieth century tended to be simpler. Still important, however, were the accessories: headpieces, gloves, shoes, and flowers.

Photos and other memorabilia can help us correctly determine bridal fashion trends. By studying the styles of women's clothing, we can approximately date a bridal picture. One image or one artifact, however, does not a trend make. But discovering, for example, a large, flamboyant 1920s headpiece and then finding another similar or matching design may well prove a trend rather than present evidence of something unique or custom made.

Of course, trends pass. Fads come and go. Economics, popular culture, and even politics can shape fashion trends. But regardless of trends, brides have long loved their dresses, and in these pages we will look at the fashions—and trends—that shaped bridal couture of the early twentieth century.

In bridal fashion, what's old is new again as ideas of the past are reinterpreted. Readers of these pages will find ideas for today's bridal gowns and headpieces while they examine the evolution of bridal fashions.

Opposite: Alice and Michael Krainz were married in Cleveland, Ohio, in November 1933. The bride's headpiece is typical of the 1930s.

1900–1910: THE AGE OF INNOCENCE AND EDWARDIAN FASHION

A T THE BEGINNING OF THE 1900s, the mood in America was one of optimism. The Industrial Revolution was in full swing, and America was rapidly changing from a country of mainly agriculture to one that was mostly industrial. The economy was booming, fueled by American manufacturing.

This decade became known as the Age of Optimism, the Age of Confidence, or the Age of Innocence. Americans had great pride and confidence in themselves and their country. And they had good reason. There was a surplus in the national treasury. Daily life was being made easier and more enjoyable through new inventions and technologies.

Electricity was just one of those inventions that were changing lives. Used in industry since the late 1800s, electricity started making inroads into daily life in the early twentieth century. Homes were being wired for electricity. Electric streetcars and railroads were replacing horse-drawn vehicles in larger cities. Automobiles, then called "horseless carriages," were still considered a novelty. Autos were strictly for the rich because they were expensive to buy and keep running. While many American inventors were focusing on developing automobiles, some were looking to the skies. Wilbur and Orville Wright had their first, albeit brief, air flight in 1903. However, air flight was not given serious consideration. It was viewed as an interesting experiment, but nothing more.

This was called the Edwardian era, with mores and fashion harkening to the norms of England. Queen Victoria died in 1901, ending the Victorian era. She was succeeded by Edward VII, launching the Edwardian era. This was a time of formality between the sexes. Roles for men and women were very clearly spelled out by society. A man was expected to tip his hat to a lady. A woman was expected to be chaperoned if she was with a man who was not her husband.

Edwardian fashions favored the mature woman, accenting a wasp-thin waistline, full bosom, and ample hips and behind. The corset was a garment no woman would have considered going without. At the beginning of this decade, the corset was called the "S" corset because it forced a woman's body

Opposite: Bertha Panke and Henry Gauger pose on their wedding day in Chicago, c. 1907. The bride wears an unusual circular floral headpiece and floral greens on her dress.

into a very unnatural S-shaped posture. The bosom was thrust forward, and the hips were thrust back.

The most recognizable characteristics of Edwardian dresses are long, flowing skirts that draped gracefully over the hips, with the fullness at the back, and ended at a ruffle or small train. Skirts were worn to the floor; seeing a lady's ankles was considered improper. The bodice characteristically

This bride wears a typical Edwardian-style wedding dress with its blousy front, high neckline, and flowing skirt.

had a high neckline, fullness at the front, and a waistline that dropped forward at the front. The puff at the front of the bodice was often exaggerated with rows of ruffles or lace. Sleeves were often full and accented by lace ruffles, ending anywhere from the elbow to the wrist at a snug band or ruffle. Sometimes this snug band extended from the elbow to the wrist.

A bride at this time was expected to create an image of modesty by being entirely covered up, from her high neckline to her gloves and all the way down to her ankles. Edwardian bridal dresses were made from chiffon over satin or thin cotton muslin over heavier cotton or silk. Lace or embroidered sheer fabrics were often used to create a lighter bodice top, while still maintaining propriety. Either worn alone or over another fabric, lace fabrics were very popular for bridal gowns. There were many underlying layers to the dresses to create the fashionable shape. Bodices often had boned linings, even though the outside look was blousy. Even the skirts had many underlying shaped petticoats, with ruffles on the bottom, to create the look.

Bridal gowns of the time were usually hand-sewn. At the beginning of the 1900s, the ready-to-wear industry was in its infancy. Before this time, a woman would have made all of her own clothes or hired a dressmaker to do it for her. The rich would have had the gown custom made. Brides on a budget had to make their own. Being able to walk into a store to buy a dress was progress.

Around 1905, department stores in large cities started advertising a ready-to-wear style called a "lingerie" dress, made of lightweight fabric such

Far left: These "lingerie" dresses, advertised in Sears, Roebuck & Company's 1908 catalog, were made of "net" or silk, decorated with embroidery, lace, and insertions, and available in light pink, light blue, and white.

Left: A woman wearing a ready-made "lingerie" dress, which many budget-minded brides wore as their wedding dress.

This bride's dress from 1904 is sheer fabric with rows of short ruffles, full sleeves, and typical puffy bodice.
This may be a ready-made "lingerie" dress used as a wedding gown.

as thin, cotton muslin, with high neck and full sleeves and decorated with rows of tucks, embroidery, and lace. Although available in many pastel colors, the lingerie dress in white made it the perfect choice for an economical wedding gown for middle- to lower-class brides on a budget. Even Sears, Roebuck & Company's catalog carried lingerie dresses, so women in small towns and rural America could mail order a ready-made dress in time for their wedding day.

Especially popular were two-piece lingerie dresses, with separate bodices and skirts. After the wedding, the new bride could wear the pieces separately to the many parties and family visits she was expected to attend. Most brides of the Edwardian era wore their wedding dresses to formal affairs after they were married. Very few could afford a "one-time only" dress.

The lingerie dress also was considered appropriate for the maid of honor and bridesmaids to wear, often with the addition of a wide ribbon sash at the waist and a brooch on the collar. They, too, wore this popular style of dress in white as part of the wedding party. The lingerie dress was indeed a very useful dress in the Edwardian lady's closet.

A proper Edwardian lady wore both gloves and a hat anytime she was outside her home. Wedding gloves were long or short depending on the length of the sleeve, the goal being for the bride's arms to be totally covered. Occasionally, a bride would wear fingerless mitts, which were gloves without the fingers. This made it easier to put on the wedding band, as well as easier to handle things. Many brides also wore a brooch on the high collar.

Just as brides wore white, bridal flowers during this decade also were usually white. White roses were called "bridal" roses. Other flowers frequently used were white orchids, lilies of the valley, and orange blossoms. Queen Victoria used orange blossoms for her wedding in 1840, and this started a tradition for brides to wear or carry orange blossoms. Orange blossoms worn on bridal headpieces were usually made of wax, and very few have survived. A popular bridal bouquet fashion of the time was the "waterfall," so named for the ribbons with small flower buds hanging from the bouquet. Bridesmaids carried white flowers, too. Brides often carried prayer books adorned with several small flowers dangling from long ribbons.

Contemporary hat styles influenced bridal headpiece fashion. Hats at this time balanced atop a lady's upswept hair, giving the illusion that the hat was floating, but they were anchored to the lady's hair by large, straight hat pins. Trimmings often were chiffon, tulle, and soft feathers that were large in proportion to the brim and often obscured it. Hat decorations often were made of silk flowers, sometimes a whole bouquet. Such large hats were the norm, not the exception. Bridal veils and headpieces were not that large, but they, too, balanced atop a lady's upswept hair.

At the beginning of the 1900s, skirts were gored. That means they were made of triangular pieces of fabric with the widest side at the bottom to create fullness at the floor while maintaining a slim line over the hips. These skirts were often longer at the back to create a small train. In time, the fullness at the back was eliminated and the skirts were simply gathered at the waist. Then the skirts morphed into a simple A-line style without a lot of fullness or gathers around the waist. Trains soon disappeared from everyday dresses and began to disappear from bridal gowns, too.

Some brides wore gowns made of a thin, soft fabric like chiffon over a more solid fabric. In keeping with the fashions, the bodice was puffy with the shape exaggerated by a long, soft ruffle. Full sleeves extended to below the elbows, where they became tight, and ended in a lace ruffle at the wrist. Tight, short gloves fitted under the ends of the sleeves, keeping the bride's hands and arms entirely covered. Waistlines were accented by stiff belts with

As the size of hats grew larger as the decade progressed, more and more floral or feather decorations were used.

This Edwardian bride from Chicago has a dress of lace fabric, wide, lace ruffles, elbow-length sleeves, and a simple headpiece of flowers with two layers of veil.

a downward point at the front while skirts were made of soft, gauzy layers with bands of horizontal tucking and lace inserts for decoration.

Like brides at any time in history, Edwardian brides liked to keep mementoes of their weddings. They saved their wedding announcements, flowers from their bouquets, and even parts of their wedding gowns and veils. They put them into scrapbooks, small keepsake boxes, and shadow

boxes. Such boxes often contained a photo of the bride and groom surrounded by the bride's veil and headpiece.

Of course, trends change, and this was the case for the Edwardian bride as well. About 1907, the lady's corset changed shape, and so did

Opposite:
This very rare
Edwardian wedding
memories shadow
box of a bride and
groom c. 1906
showcases the
bride's veil and
headpiece around
the couple's
wedding photo.

Frances and
Louis Spehek,
the author's
grandparents,
were married in
Cleveland, Ohio,
on July 4, 1908.
The bride's slightly
gathered skirt
indicates the
change in fashion
in 1907.

13

These four ladies are a good example of the changes in the fashionable silhouette c. 1907 when skirts became less full and simpler.

This elegant bridal couple was photographed in Chicago in about 1908. The dress style shows the change away from the Edwardian style.

the fashionable silhouette. The bosom and hips were no longer emphasized. Skirts became plainer and less full, eventually assuming the A-line shape. Bodices were no longer as puffy, either, even though the necklines were still high and the sleeves remained full. About this time, the hemline came up an inch or two also.

Toward the end of the decade, many brides favored simple dresses, with only embroidery decoration. Bodices were embroidered, and skirts often featured two bands of embroidery that extended down from the waistline to the horizontal band of embroidery near the bottom. Full sleeves were gathered at the elbow and ended there in a wide lace ruffle. Gloves remained popular, and many brides continued to wear elbow-length, fingerless mitts. Simplicity extended to the headpiece, which often was made of tightly ruffled veil netting and small white flowers, likely wax orange blossoms. Brides of this time often carried simple bouquets with a few flowers, plenty of greenery, and a wide white satin ribbon hanging down. Some brides also wore boutonnieres on their bodices.

By the end of the decade, bridal fashion shifted from the blousy look to gowns decorated with satin revers, or flat panels, with lace overlay and edged in lace. High satin collars were adorned with lace ruffle edging and reached

This Milwaukee, Wisconsin, bride's dress is satin with embroidered edges and waistband in a style that was popular near the end of the decade.

15

almost up to the ears. Rows of thin tucking often decorated the top of the sleeves, which had moderate fullness. Skirts featured a thin fabric over a satin slip with white embroidery down the center front and a satin band near the bottom. Popular headpieces looked like solid tiaras, decorated with pearls and two lengths of veil, the longer veil dragging on the floor. Another style of typical headpiece consisted of bunches of flowers, net ruffling, and a single-layer veil that trailed to the ground.

Near the end of this decade, bridal fashion took on a more severe look. The puffy bodice look gave way to a fit that was closer to the bride's body, with a neckline without lace edging. Satin gowns often featured a few bands of white embroidery. The satin bands, or revers, on the bodice ended at the waist. The bodice between the revers and the high collar often was made of a sheer, embroidered fabric.

An ornate bridal gown decorated with white silk fringe, ribbon rosette, tassels, and embroidery on a bride from Chicago.

Bouquets at the end of the decade often featured white roses and white lilies of the valley with gauzy white ribbons. The bouquet waterfall also consisted of small bunches of lilies of the valley tied to the bottoms of sheer ribbons.

Although the dress style became more severe, bridal dresses could still be ornately decorated with satin ribbon rosettes and silk tassels. Bodices often were embroidered, up to and including the high neckline collar. Bands of embroidery and silk fringe decorated the skirts. Sleeves were tight, ending with a band of embroidery and silk fringe.

At the end of the decade, bridesmaids often wore dresses with bodices with revers in a V, the space between them a sheer, embroidered fabric, with high neck with ruffled edge. Some bridesmaids' gowns featured jewel necklines and rows of ruffles on the bodice.

Bridesmaids often wore flowers in their hair, carried bouquets made of mixed flowers, and pinned boutonnieres on their bodices.

Fashion evolved during the Age of Innocence, a time before radio and television became widespread entertainment and celebrities held such sway over our lives. Instead, people watched actual live performers in vaudeville or made their own entertainment such as playing music at home. The movie industry was just starting, and movies were silent, black and white, and very short. This new technology was just one of the many that had Americans excited about the future.

All in all, life was looking good for most Americans at the end of the first decade of the twentieth century. They had hope that their lives would continue to get better and become more comfortable. All the new inventions and technologies were exciting. Americans felt like they were making progress. The future looked good.

This large bridal party, c. 1909, features bridesmaids wearing two different styles of dress, some with low necklines.

1910–1920: INNOCENCE, OPTIMISM, AND THE GOOD LIFE

THE AGE OF INNOCENCE that began in the previous decade continued into the second decade of the twentieth century. Economic growth continued, and mass production was allowing more Americans to experience "the good life."

Automobiles were quickly replacing the horse as a means of transportation. Henry Ford introduced the Model T in 1908, and in 1911, replaced the wooden body with metal. The Model T was soon dubbed the "Tin Lizzie."

On April 10, 1912, the RMS *Titanic* set sail from England for New York City on her maiden voyage, with 2,223 people enjoying the luxury liner. *Titanic* epitomized opulence and luxury, and was considered unsinkable. Everyone had confidence in the technologies of the day, but on April 14, 1912, she hit an iceberg and sank. With lifeboats for only 1,178 people— not nearly enough for all the people on board—1,517 people lost their lives in the cold Atlantic waters.

Just as technology was changing, so was fashion. Women's dresses at the beginning of this decade were not frilly or flowing like those of ten years earlier. Waists were no longer expected to be artificially tiny. The old S-shaped corsets were being replaced with straight corsets that accepted the size of a woman's waist. Bodices were no longer super-blousy, and skirts created an A-line shape reaching almost to the floor.

Waistlines hit at the natural waist or slightly above, while the bodice featured only a slight pouch. Middy-style bodices were often worn with high-necked blouses underneath. The collar was a striped fabric. The buttons on the bodice were repeated on the skirt. Gowns often featured a wide, gathered satin cummerbund around the waist that matched satin cuffs. It was customary to wear a lady's watch pinned to the bodice.

In about 1910, Parisian fashion designer Paul Poiret became strongly influenced by Oriental designs, silks, and colors. He incorporated into his designs the Japanese kimono and obi, the wide band that goes around the waist to hold the kimono closed. Following his fashion influence, many

Opposite:
This version of a bridal cap was made of net attached to a wire frame to cover the whole top of the head and decorated by small bunches of wax orange blossoms.

This Toledo, Ohio, bride is photographed in about 1912 wearing a "fashion-forward" bridal gown in the kimono style made popular by French designer Poiret.

American dresses between 1910 and 1914 featured a V neckline, created by two pieces of fabric that met or overlapped just above the bust, giving the bodice the look of a kimono top. Just below the bust was a wide band almost to the waist, looking like an obi. These were either tightly gathered or plain with a large flat bow similar to an obi back.

"Fashion-forward" bridal gowns in Poiret's kimono style were popular among American brides in the early 1910s. Dresses of this style were often

made in lightweight chiffon and featured bodices with short sleeves with an overlay of sheer fabric, edged in lace, covering the shoulders and gathered into a high waistline. Gathered ruching typically extended from the bust to the waist representing the Oriental obi. Skirts often were one layer gathered at the waist, with a train at the back. Despite the fashion-forward design, modesty remained important, and brides often wore long gloves that reached up to the edge of the dress sleeves.

For some modern brides, large hats gave way to puffy caps edged in silk orange blossoms. Long veils acted as trains, and large bouquets were adorned with silk waterfalls made of ribbons. Shoes most often white and low-heeled, some with large rosettes on the toes.

Bridesmaids also embraced modern styles, including the kimono. Bodices on bridesmaids' gowns often featured a loose lace layer over a solid fabric. A wide, gathered cummerbund in a silky, solid, colored fabric fit around the waist. Popular skirts consisted of three layers in the tunic style: a short lace layer over a sheer chiffon layer over the satin bottom layer.

Below, left: Satin was often used on the collar, cummerbund, and cuffs of dresses of the early 1910s. Buttons were also used as decorations.

Below right: This bride wears another version of the kimono-style dress, with a flat bow in front just below her bust, representing the Oriental obi.

Right: This bridal couple was married in Elgin, Illinois. The bride's dress has chiffon panels over the skirt to create the tunic look. Her bouquet has loosely opened roses and fern greenery tied by a ribbon of veil netting.

Below: These tunic dresses appeared in *Needlecraft* magazine in October 1914. The dress on the right is for dressy occasions, and the other is for outside the home.

The kimono look came in variations. Some bridal parties wore wide cummerbunds with a large, flat bow in front tied just below the bust. The bodice featured a thin, net-like fabric on top of the heavier bodice fabric. It covered the front of the bodice and shoulders like a shawl and crossed in front, in the kimono style. Plain sleeves ended at the elbow, often in a lace edging. Though they generally remained popular accessories, some modern brides chose to forgo gloves, even though doing so may have been daring for the times.

Bridal fashion and designer gowns shaped women's fashion for everyday wear. Designer evening dresses in 1912 were in a cylinder-shaped silhouette or sheath. The fabric was soft and flowed around the body. The waistline was high, just below the bust. The top was often a tunic that reached almost to the knees, over a long narrow underskirt that reached to the floor. This produced a high-waisted silhouette with a widening at the hips, which narrowed again at the ankles.

This look was translated into everyday wear with the tunic dress. The waistline hit at the natural waist or above. One or two layers of overskirt hanging over a narrow underskirt was sometimes called the "hobble" skirt because it was so narrow that a woman could take only small steps. In January 1912, an Elgin, Illinois, newspaper reported that motormen and conductors on the streetcars claimed that the hobble skirt was delaying service because women wearing this fashion were taking too long to get on and off the cars.

This illustration is from *Needlecraft* magazine, August 1916. These dress patterns represent a change in fashion to a softer, fuller skirt.

The tunic look influenced both women's fashion in general and bridal gowns. Everyday skirts often had a two- or three-tiered effect, with scalloped edges. Sometimes the tunic look was in the form of separate panels hanging down over the underskirt.

Some tunic dresses featured simple, floor-length skirts made of soft chiffon. The bodice often was of an overlap surplice style edged in an embroidered satin band. This band often repeated on the skirt tunic layer that came to a downward point in the front. A satin embroidered fabric filled in the V neckline of the bodice. Long sleeves featured horizontal pin tucks at the top.

Bridal gowns were often made of sheer, soft fabric decorated with embroidery on the skirt's layers as well as the bodice. In a departure from the floor-length dresses and veils that had long been popular, some brides

A new style of hat became fashionable around 1912. The brim was much smaller, and the hat sat lower on the head.

accessorized their look with veils that reached just to the edge of the skirt, sometimes above the ankle.

By 1916, fashion was dictating a softer, gathered tunic with a wider underskirt. The hobble underskirt disappeared. The natural waist was back in vogue, too. The whole look was softer and more feminine. This change also was reflected in dress sewing patterns.

Typical bridal fashions for the middle of the 1910s included bridal gowns in a soft fabric with embroidery on the bodice. Puffy bridal caps of net, worn low on the head and edged in small flowers, also were popular. Brides often wore long veils attached to the back of the cap.

This Milwaukee, Wisconsin, bride wears a ring of lace and flowers encircling her head and producing the look of a bridal cap, with her veil attached at the back. Her bouquet consists of carnations and fern greenery.

Bridesmaids of the day often favored kimono-style or tunic-style dresses. Sheer fabric over underdresses, square necklines, short sleeves, and scalloped hems also were popular.

This Chicago bride wears another style of bridal cap covering the top of her head, and decorated by a band of flowers.

25

From bouquets to jewelry to shoes, accessories were important for the bride of the 1910s. Bridal bouquets were often rather large, made of roses or peonies and baby's breath with multiple flowers on streamers. The women of the bridal party typically wore white shoes with about 1.5-inch heels and white stockings.

At the start of the decade, extremely wide-brimmed hats were still considered fashionable and widely worn. Around 1912, though, hat styles began to change. Brims got smaller, crowns got higher, and hats sat much lower on the head. Wearing hats low on the head was to remain fashionable into the 1920s.

The change in style of headwear was reflected in bridal headpieces, marking the emergence of the bridal cap, a concoction of net, wire, lace, and flowers that covered the bride's head. Many such caps featured small bunches of orange blossoms attached to the front and sides while a gathered veil was attached at the back. Other caps featured a ring of lace and flowers, again with the veil attached at the back. In fact, there were many variations of the bridal cap. One popular version gathered around the bride's head with a circlet of flowers, probably orange blossoms. Some bridal caps were puffy and loosely covered the head, gathered in a circle around her head, causing the edge to form a ruffle.

This Milwaukee, Wisconsin, bride wears a puffy bridal cap that loosely covers her head. She also wears a cloth shawl over her dress.

As today, fashion in the early twentieth century took its influence from many directions. During the 1910s, silent movies progressed from being a novelty to become one of the most popular forms of entertainment in America. Moviegoers became fans of actors such as comics Charlie Chaplin and Roscoe "Fatty" Arbuckle, cowboy stars Tom Mix and William S. Hart, and the swashbuckling hero of adventure films Douglas Fairbanks.

The movie queen was a new phenomenon in America. Some actresses who symbolized the romantic ideas of America were Mary Pickford, known as "Little Mary, America's Sweetheart," the romantic heroine; Theda Bara "The Vamp," the wicked siren with kohl-rimmed eyes and long, black hair; and sisters Lillian and Dorothy Gish, the fragile innocents. Girls and young women all over America tried to copy their hairstyles, clothes, and especially their ways with men. What happened on the movie screen was changing culture and fashion. What would become a long-term phenomenon of heavy pop culture influence was just beginning.

When World War I erupted in Europe in August 1914, most Americans were surprised. Up until then, their attitude had been one of isolationism: Europe was far away and couldn't affect them. It took a while after the *Lusitania* was sunk for Congress and President Woodrow Wilson to declare war on Germany on April 6, 1917.

And so the young men marched off to war—and the women marched off to fill the manpower gap. Women found work in shipyards, ammunitions factories, and many other wartime industries. Although not allowed in combat during World War I, thousands of American women served in the military performing many noncombat duties such as clerical work.

Influenced by the war, women's clothing of the mid- to late-1910s trended to a more severe, military look, featuring skirts wider at the hem, often with soft pleats and a hemline as much as six inches from the ground. Braiding, large patch pockets, and buckled belts reflected the military styling.

After the war, designers rapidly made a change in the fashionable look. The style became one of ease and liberation from past restrictions. The chemise, a straight, loose sheath hanging from the shoulders and belted at the waist, became the new style. Skirt lengths stopped about midcalf. The chemise was a far cry from the restrictive dress styles popular at the beginning of the 1900s.

As World War I was nearing its end, a more deadly enemy appeared: a worldwide influenza epidemic in 1918. This virus killed America's young and healthy, and then was carried to Europe with American troops. It eventually killed an estimated 50 million people across the world, which was millions more than died in World War I.

Understandably, by the time The Great War ended on November 11, 1918, most young people did not have much hope for the future. Between the influenza epidemic and the war, they were not even sure they had a future, adopting the attitude of "live-for-today-because-you-might-not-have-a-tomorrow."

At a time when Americans needed to have their spirits raised or have a good time, Prohibition was voted in on January 29, 1919, making it illegal to sell, distribute, or even consume alcohol. This would have extreme consequences in the 1920s.

After the cranked-up emotions of wartime, those who returned from the war experienced a letdown, with feelings of cynicism and negativity. By the end of the decade, American optimism had turned into pessimism. All of the energy, enthusiasm, and idealism of the 1910s had died in World War I. The Age of Innocence was gone for good.

1920–1930: THE JAZZ AGE AND FLAPPER FASHION

THE YEARS BETWEEN 1920 and 1930 have been called the Roaring Twenties, the Flapper Era, the Jazz Age, and the Lawless Decade. It was during this decade, under the laws of Prohibition, that the sale and manufacture of beer, wine, whiskey, and all other alcoholic beverages were illegal.

The beginning of the 1920s found Americans shocked by the devastation of World War I's 10 million military personnel killed and the influenza epidemic that killed 50 million more people around the world. American optimism and idealism had vanished. A whole generation embodied an "eat-drink-and-be-merry-for-tomorrow-we-may-die" attitude, wanting to reclaim their youth and the partying missed while fighting the war. People wanted to forget the past few years and have fun. Their war nerves craved speed, excitement, and passion; settling down was not going to be possible.

Unfortunately, on January 16, 1920, Prohibition, the 18th Amendment to the Constitution, became law, a well-meaning law that ended up having extremely negative effects on America in more ways than one. While legitimate bars were forced to close, illegal "speakeasies" opened in every city and neighborhood, patronized by people who had never even thought of going into a bar before Prohibition. To stock these speakeasies, alcohol was smuggled into the United States or brewed at home. Gangsters saw an opportunity and took over the smuggling and distribution of alcohol. This was the start of organized crime in America, and gang warfare eventually led to a climate of lawlessness.

As the economy finally started booming again, the lives of most Americans were changed by the new inventions of radio and electrical appliances such as toasters, washing machines, and many other conveniences. The percentage of homes with electricity rose from only 20 percent in 1919 to 63 percent in 1927.

Automobiles were becoming less expensive, well within the price range of middle-class Americans, resulting in an increase in the number of cars on the road. Cars provided average people with a freedom and individuality that was not possible before. Families could travel in their own vehicles instead of relying on public transportation.

Opposite:
In 1922, the British archaeologist Howard Carter discovered the tomb of Egyptian King Tutankamen. "Tutmania" may have inspired this bride's headpiece, which was made of a net crown on a frame with pleated lace standing out around the head.

World War I had accelerated the development of air flight from the novelty of short-distance, primitive flying machines to more reliable airplanes capable of carrying heavier loads and passengers and flying greater distances. Increased capabilities of airplanes drew daring aviators trying to set new distance and speed records. The most famous of these were Charles Lindbergh, who was the first pilot to fly solo nonstop across the Atlantic Ocean, from New York to Paris, in May 1927, in *The Spirit of St. Louis*, and female aviator Amelia Earhart, who would eventually disappear, in 1937, on an around-the-world flight.

Although Earhart launched fashion trends and even had her own clothing line, it was Prohibition that most deeply impacted American culture. Prohibition had a far-reaching effect on American morals, especially on those in their twenties and thirties. Now that alcohol was illegal, drinking a cocktail became a very exciting adventure, a thrill, fueling a youthful rebellion.

In earlier decades, society had expected young ladies to be prim and proper, modest, and, above all,

Above: This bridesmaid wears a typical sheath dress from the beginning of the 1920s with the fashionable band around her head.

Right: Even though the straight look was in, it was not flattering on every figure.

Opposite, top: This short hairstyle was typical for the late 1920s. The waves are called "finger waves" and were set by hand and held in place with long clips until the hair dried.

virtuous. Young men were supposed to be industrious and hardworking, conservative in their actions. World War I had an extreme impact on these attitudes. Europeans had more sophisticated attitudes, openly drinking and smoking in outdoor cafes. They also had a more casual attitude toward sex. Young American men and women who had served in Europe were exposed to those ideas and brought them home to America. They were changed, and they also changed those around them as the youths at home eagerly adopted these new ideas. There was no going back to Victorian and Edwardian mores.

Not only were social attitudes being influenced by Europe, but so too were women's fashions. Head-hugging cloche hats, short dresses, face make-up, silk stockings, long strings of beads, and "bobbed" hair were all the rage. Strangest of all was the fashion of wearing unbuckled galoshes, rubberized rain boots that flapped when the fashionable woman walked. These flapping galoshes inspired the term "Flapper" associated with fashion-forward gals.

All these changes shocked and upset conservative America. Fathers, grandparents, husbands, and even ministers were scandalized by women showing their legs as hemlines steadily moved upward, almost to the knees. Before the 1920s, a flash of ankle had been considered risqué.

Below:
This collection of wedding dress patterns, sold by McCall's in 1921, was patterned after the evening dress styles of the time.

They were equally outraged when women cut their long hair. Only the most daring young women cut their hair short all at once. Many women started out slowly by having just the front hair shortened, keeping the back long and in a bun, giving the men in their lives time to get adjusted to the new look. Before long these women realized that it was easier to care for shorter hair, and soon shortened their back hair, too. Once their hair was short, they learned to do the fashionable finger waves and make their hairstyles more individual, often copying the hairstyle of their favorite actress. By the middle of the decade, many women were wearing a style called the Shingle, which was head hugging, very short in back with longer hair at the sides that formed a curl on the cheek.

During the 1920s, Americans flocked to the movies to see silent films. Besides going to be entertained, people went to be inspired by what they saw on the screen. Movies taught people how to dress, how to act tough, how to talk to the opposite sex, how to walk provocatively, how to smoke, and, more importantly, how to appear sexy.

The music of the decade was jazz—erratic, fast, feverish, and exciting; real American music that combined elements of ragtime, marching band music, and blues. Jazz inspired scandalous new dances that went by names like the "Black Bottom" and the "Charleston." It was an expression of the times: energetic, breathless, and active.

This bridal headpiece has three decorative bands with white three-dimensional "leaves," probably of wax, and pleated netting sticking up in back.

Flapper styles represented more than just fashion changes; they symbolized the new morality for the younger generation. Elders still supported the old Victorian moral code whereby women were expected to be the guardians of morality and young girls should remain innocent. Smoking and drinking were totally forbidden for girls. But during the 1920s, these old rules were rejected as old-fashioned and prudish, and fashion symbolized that rejection.

To be able to dance and move, Flapper dresses were usually thin, sleeveless, open-necked, and loose fitting, often decorated with fringe to accentuate their movements. The wilder girls even rolled down their silk stockings to below their knees, scandalously revealing their knees and shins. They also abandoned their corsets. If mothers insisted their daughters wear a corset to a dance, the girls quickly stopped in the ladies room and removed it before the fun began.

Although not every young woman was a Flapper, their extremes of dress influenced fashion in general. The thin, adolescent, boyish, or "garçonne," look became fashionable, in sharp contrast to earlier decades when the mature, well-rounded woman's body was considered stylish and when fat was thought to indicate wealth. Corsets changed from stiffly boned contraptions that molded a woman's body into an hour-glass shape into softer elastic versions that flattened the breasts and hips for a boyish look.

That look carried over to bridal parties. The early 1920s bridesmaid often wore a loose, scoop-necked dress of a soft shiny fabric, elbow-length sleeves, slightly gathered skirt, and net sash around the waist. Also common was a band around her head of the same netting, with a bow in back.

At the beginning of the 1920s, the fashionable dress was a tube-shaped sheath that hung from the shoulders with a loose sash around the natural waistline. As the decade went on, the waistline of the dress moved downward to the hips and stayed there. Everyday dresses started looking more like big rectangles with the print of the fabric or any applied decoration as the focus. This simplification of dress styles made the manufacture of dresses easier, resulting in an increase in ready-to-wear clothing. Home sewing grew in popularity as pattern companies such as McCall's offered patterns for the average woman.

This St. Louis, Missouri, bride wears a headpiece reflecting the Arab-sheik fashion inspired by Rudolph Valentino in the movie *The Sheik*.

With this simpler, straight look, accessories became more important. Though gloves still covered the hands, legs were in full view, often from the knee down. Old-fashioned high-top shoes were out, and silk stockings with more open shoes were in. A popular shoe style had medium-height thick heels with a single or T-strap fastening across the foot. Many brides of this decade wore this style of shoe.

Couture, evening, and party dresses during this time, however, favored slightly fuller skirts made of gathered fabric, soft tiers, or triangular godet inserts. Also popular were full sashes that wrapped around the hips with one end longer and touching the ground. A variation was to attach extra fabric sashes to one or both hips and let them drape down the straight skirt. Flowers or beaded accents were often worn on one hip. Another fashionable look was having a skirt longer in back than in front. The most recognizable evening dress style from this era was the thin, net dress heavily decorated with glass and steel beads over a satin slip.

When it came to wedding dresses, fashion seemed to follow the styles of evening and party dresses, instead of the tubular, everyday look. Bodices were usually plain with a scoop neckline, dropped waistline, and slightly full skirt. Skirt lengths ranged from midcalf to just below the knee. Skirt variations were two or three tiers of gathered lace, scalloped taffeta, gathered crepe with horizontal satin bands, glass bugle bead patterns on sheer chiffon, pointed hems, and skirts longer in back than front. As wedding dresses got simpler, headpieces

This bride wears a headpiece made of sections heavily encrusted with beads and pearls and netting, plus a very long veil that created her train.

and bouquets got larger and more ornate; and as wedding dresses got shorter, veils got longer, creating a train effect. Fabrics used for bridal fashions included sheer chiffons, taffetas, and satins decorated with ribbons, beading, and lace.

The large bridal bouquets were no longer just roses, as chrysanthemums and lilies were also used. Ribbon waterfalls, with their dangling flowers buds, remained popular. Some brides accented their bouquets with a loosely woven pattern of ribbons atop the flowers.

During the first half of the 1920s, women wore a decorative band across the forehead and around the head with evening and party dresses. These headbands ranged from simple chiffon sashes to highly beaded and sequined bands with an ornate brooch, a straight feather, or an ostrich plume standing straight up. This head decoration is reflected in the bridal headpieces of the early 1920s with headbands of different materials. Puffs of tulle net were often added at the back and the veil hung down the back from there.

Clara Bow, the silent film actress, was called the "It" girl—meaning she had sex appeal and flaunted it in her movies—and quickly became an icon of sexual freedom for women in the 1920s. Girls and women imitated her mannerisms, so when she appeared wearing hats with brims so low they sat on her eyebrows, American women started wearing hats that low, too. This affected bridal fashions as headpieces inched lower and lower on the bride's head. Bridal headpieces of gathered netting on a frame edged with gathered lace and trimmed with small flowers often closely encircled the bride's face

The 1921 movie hit *The Sheik*, starring heartthrob Rudolph Valentino dressed in an Arab head dress, inspired bridal headpieces for several years. Made primarily of netting, gathered and pleated and decorated by ornate cords and wax orange blossoms across the forehead, they often featured veils with two layers edged in decorative stitching.

While jazz bands filled the speakeasies with music, and people drank and danced the night away, no one suspected that the party was about to come to an abrupt end. Wild speculation in stocks brought it all down when the stock market crashed on Black Thursday, October 24, 1929, and the Great Depression loomed.

This bride wears a headpiece of pearls on net and wire foundation on top of a puffed up veil. Her hip-level waistline is accented by ribbon bows, and her skirt has a pointed hem.

1930–1940: THE GREAT DEPRESSION

IF THE 1920s were the decade of optimism, the 1930s were the polar opposite, the decade of the Great Depression. The collapse of the stock market set off a nationwide business depression, resulting in 7 million workers losing their jobs by the end of 1930, and that number rose to 14 million by the end of 1931. As if that wasn't bad enough, five thousand banks collapsed, wiping out the life savings of millions of people.

Franklin Delano Roosevelt beat Herbert Hoover for President of the United States in 1932. FDR treated the Depression with all the emergency and immediacy of a war. He campaigned on a policy of a "New Deal" for America's "forgotten man"—the unemployed—basing his New Deal programs on what he called the three Rs: Relief, Recovery, and Reform. Not all of FDR's New Deal programs worked, and not every American supported his ideas and programs, but overall, the New Deal programs slowly pulled the country out of the severe economic and psychological depression that was the Great Depression.

The 1930s and the Great Depression left an indelible mark on the American psyche. Almost everyone has seen the black and white images of people standing in bread lines outside soup kitchens; men carrying signs that read "will work for food;" evicted families huddled on the side walk with their household belongings; whole families living in their cars with their few possessions tied on top. The psychological reaction to being ruined, or waiting to be ruined, was terror and bewilderment. No one was prepared for what was happening to them. Although not every American was out of work or homeless, those still working struggled to make ends meet, always in fear of losing what they still had.

To make matters worse, a lack of rainfall in the Midwest from 1931 to 1935 parched farmland so badly it blew away when the winds came. It was the Dust Bowl. Families lost their farms, and thousands made their way west looking for a new way to make a living. These "Okies" packed their whole families into their cars or trucks, loaded up their belongings, and started across the country.

By the 1930s, one out of every two American families owned a car, even though it most often was an old car bought in the better days of the 1920s,

Opposite: Josephine and Stanley Zalewski II were married in 1939. The bride's dress, made of chiffon, features rows of ruffles across the bodice front and back of the skirt, forming a train.

Above left:
These 1930s
women sport the
new soft, felt hats
designed to go
along with their
more flowing
dress styles.

Above right:
This bride's "boat"
neckline style
dress was popular
at the beginning
of the 1930s.
Her headpiece is
similar to styles
worn in the 1920,
just placed further
back on the head.

or a used car that had been patched up to keep it running. Most people avoided the high costs of gas, tires, and repair parts by using public transportation such as streetcars, buses, and trains.

The early 1930s were not a happy time; cynicism and despair were rampant. Crime was growing, and newspapers and newsreels made heroes out of villains by glorifying the escapades of gangsters such as Al Capone and John Dillinger. Prohibition had fueled the growth of organized crime, which took over gambling, labor racketeering, loan sharking, narcotics distribution, and prostitution after the repeal of Prohibition in 1933.

Radio and film lent some measure of escape, providing entertainment in the form of comedies, dramas, sporting events, and crime stoppers. President Roosevelt broadcast his "Fireside Chats" on the radio to reassure a frightened nation that things were improving.

As comforting as those chats were for many Americans, it was the movies that provided the most popular escape. In the dark of the theater, it was easy to leave the real world outside. Now that moving pictures had sound, musicals became a popular escape from the Depression. Actors and actresses made their mark on the culture of the day, perhaps none more so than Jean Harlow. The 1920s movie vamp was dark haired, while the "good girl" was blonde, but Jean Harlow changed all that in the new decade. Her platinum blonde hair was so unusual, and her gowns so low cut, that the term "Blonde Bombshell" was coined to describe her. Harlow's hair inspired women to bleach their hair platinum in an attempt to emulate her sexy look.

Not only did women copy the clothes and hairstyles of their favorite actresses, they also copied their on-screen behavior, language, and mannerisms. The 1920s had the flighty Flappers, but in the 1930s, a more glamorous, articulate, and independent woman became the ideal.

Even though the worsening economic depression made it increasingly difficult for women to buy new clothes, fashions still evolved. The fashions of the early 1930s were stylish and elegant, with longer flowing lines and longer skirts. Although the silhouette was still the long, lean cylinder,

Below left:
This bride's cowl-necked satin gown was typical for the early 1930s. Her creative headpiece was made of veil netting and lace.

Below right:
This Chicago bridesmaid wears a dress with triangular "godets" at the bottom, creating a flared skirt. Her headpiece, with its sheer brim, was a popular style.

The author's parents, Frances and Charles Kikel, were married on April 18, 1935, in Cleveland, Ohio. The bride's simple, satin dress has satin rose buds around the neckline.

This bride's dress uses carriage pleats over the shoulders to create both the neckline and long sleeves. The drape of her dress is broken only by the ribbon sash at her waist.

the waistline was back up at the natural waist and pattern pieces were shaped to drape gracefully over the woman's bodice and hips. In place of flat, shapeless dresses of the 1920s, designers created shape with interesting draping, seaming, and color blocking. As the economy went downward, so did the hemline. Longer, narrower skirts were either softly pleated or flared with godets near the bottom of the skirt, which now fell to the bottom of the calf.

To create this newer, flowing look, softer fabrics such as fine wools, crepes, and jerseys, for day and silk chiffons, crepes de Chine, and shiny satins for evening were cut on the diagonal. Evening dresses now reached to the floor, creating a definite distinction between day and evening wear, a new fashion idea. After wearing practical clothes all day, it was exciting for a woman to change into a totally impractical evening dress to go out. Eveningwear was worn to go to dinner, dancing, parties, or the theater.

Cutting fabric on a diagonal, or bias, produced a dress that clung around the bosom, waist, and hips and then flared out from the thighs into an elegant, flowing skirt. Bias-cut fabric draped in sinuous folds, clung where it touched the body and stretched enough to make it easy for the wearer to slip it on without any additional side, back, or front openings.

Hats changed along with dress fashions. The head-hugging, helmet-like cloche popular in the 1920s did not fit with the new more graceful styles. Hats became smaller, with rounded crowns and smaller brims sitting on top of the head, often tilted to one side.

As the 1930s progressed, the Shingle bob of the 1920s evolved into a longer, midlength style with all-over finger waves, until a long shoulder-length bob was popular by 1938. By the end of the 1930s, longer hair was often pinned up on top of the head in an upswept hairdo.

Despite the Depression, couples still fell in love and got married. To save expenses on church services and flowers, two weddings were often performed during the same church service. Wedding dresses became simpler, straighter, and much less decorated, relying mostly on the beauty of the fabric itself. Satin was popular for its sheen, and chiffon for its lightness. Roses of satin were often used to add interest to the plain gowns.

This mid-1930s bride and her bridesmaids all wear caps made of netting. The bride holds a bouquet of large lilies.

Theresa and Herb Fischer were married on May 31, 1939. Her dress, like those of her bridesmaids, reflects the change in dress styles at the end of the decade.

Necklines varied from softly draped boat-neck to pleated stand-up to low cut, and sleeves were long and slender. Long trains were abandoned by many brides, and most dresses ended at the floor, often with a flare.

Bridesmaids wore dresses made of crepe, chiffon, or velvet in styles similar to the bride's gown, with few decorations, and relying on the beauty of the fabric. Sleeves were long or short, depending on the season.

Opposite:
This well-dressed wedding party from Blue Island, Illinois, reflects the end of the Depression in 1939. Notice the length of the bride's train.

About 1932, bridal headpieces started changing from the ornate lace and bead affairs of the 1920s to small hats creatively made of bridal veil netting. Brides often wore hats with stand-up brims made of two layers of folded-over, starched netting sewn onto veil netting in an egg shape. The results looked like small hats. Designers were creative in their use of materials to make and decorate these bridal hats, even adding wax orange blossoms. Bridesmaids wore this style of hat, too, often with sheer brims. To replace the train, the veil was long and often decorated with lace edging.

Some 1930s fashions continued to use godets at the bottom of the skirt, which led to a flared hemline. Creating sleeves with one or two layers of soft ruffles around the armhole was another popular 1930s style.

As the Depression ground on, bridal bouquets got smaller, and the ribbon and rose bud waterfall was eliminated. Brides also started substituting cheaper flowers in place of the expensive bridal roses. Chrysanthemums,

shasta daisies, baby's breath, and lilies of the valley were used more frequently, along with a lot of greenery for fill.

Just before the start of World War II in 1939 there was a short-lived change in fashion, from the flowing style of the 1930s to a more structured dress with nipped-in waist and fuller skirt. Fabrics changed, too, and lace over a solid fabric became popular. Necklines often were high with small, folded-back collars, and skirts became fuller with trains. The style of headpieces changed, also, to a band of flowers and plain veil. Many bridesmaids' dresses had gathered, beribboned, scoop-necked bodices with short puffy sleeves, gathered cummerbund, and softly gathered long skirt.

A starched lace cap and jacket-style dress with a very long train was not unusual. Bridesmaids' long dresses featured sheet lace over a solid fabric, high necklines with small, folded down collars, and two layers of ruffle for sleeves. They often wore starched caps decorated with fabric flowers and short veils.

By the end of the 1930s, the threat of the Depression was not as great as the rise to power in Germany of Adolf Hitler and the Nazi Party. The decade had started in a Depression and would end in a war with the start of World War II. Countries gearing up for the coming war served to bring an end to the Depression. World War II started in 1939 with Hitler's invasion of Poland, while in America the "World of Tomorrow" World's Fair opened in Flushing, New York. Despite what was going on in the world, America hoped to remain neutral and stay out of the conflict.

The bridesmaids in this wedding party wear caps of satin and velvet with short veils behind. The bride's lace dress has a long train

44

1940–1950: WAR, RECOVERY, AND CHANGING TRENDS

ALTHOUGH World War II began in 1939 when Germany invaded Poland, America did not enter the war until December 8, 1941, after Japan bombed Pearl Harbor. The attack on Pearl Harbor generated enough anger, fear, and hatred to unite Americans more strongly than at any time in history.

Once war was declared, the federal government was given the power to allocate raw materials, establish priorities for production, and ration supplies. Basically, the government told businesses what to make, set production quotas for them, and could even take over plants if those quotas were not met.

Below: This lovely bride wears a mid-1940s bridal dress style with shoulder emphasis and short lace peplum attached at the waistline.

Above: This typical "Utility" dress pattern fit into the L-85 restrictions on clothing during the war. Dresses typically had broad shoulders, slender bodices, and A-line skirts.

45

Above left:
The bride wears
her good dress
and hat, and so
does the
bridesmaid, in
this 1942
wartime wedding.

Above right: This
Downers Grove,
Illinois, bride
wears her good
dress, matching
puffed net
headpiece,

While World War II raged, the home front became another battleground in the war as Americans accepted shortages of consumer products, adhered to rationing restrictions, bought war bonds, and worked overtime to produce the weapons and supplies needed by the troops. Conducting the war required huge amounts of petroleum, steel, rubber tires, wool, and other vital raw materials, as well as meat, bread, butter, coffee, and other foodstuffs. This resulted in food rationing at home as the nation struggled to feed not only American troops but Allied soldiers and the victims of the war in Europe as well.

Government rationing of tires and gasoline drastically reduced driving. With no new cars being manufactured, people were challenged with keeping their cars patched and running. Ride sharing was one solution, and mass transportation was another as people jammed into buses and trains.

Rationing was complicated and confusing for both shoppers and merchants. Each person, adults and children alike, was issued a ration book with stamps worth various points that authorized them to buy scarce items. Once people used up their stamps for such items as meat and gasoline, they were out of luck because they could not buy more without the proper ration stamps. The average gasoline ration was three gallons per week, the yearly butter ration was twelve pounds per person (25 percent less than normal), and new leather shoes were restricted to three pairs per year.

Because of the war effort, unemployment fell drastically and workers earned higher wages than they had in years. The jobs created by the war gave people money to spend for the first time in years since to the Great Depression, but with rationing and shortages, it was impossible to buy what they desired. Subsistence living, which had started during the Depression, continued throughout the war.

With so many men off to war, women stepped in to fill the labor shortages, with 7 million of them joining the workforce during the war. "Rosie the Riveter" symbolized these women, who helped to build the planes, tanks, ships, and guns that fought the war. World War II gave women the opportunity to hold traditionally male jobs such as miners, meat packers, cab drivers, lumberjacks, welders, and even railroad workers. To do these jobs, women began wearing slacks to work, starting a fashion trend. They also wore scarves on their heads to keep their hair out of the machinery.

Although women were not allowed to fight as soldiers, in 1942 the Women's Army Corps (WAC), the Navy's Women Accepted for Volunteer Emergency Service (WAVES), and the Women's Air Force Service Pilots (WASP) were created to allow women to fly planes, drive trucks, nurse the sick and wounded, and perform other noncombat jobs, freeing men for combat.

Fashion was greatly influenced by World War II. Paris had long been the source of fashion trends before the war. But when the Germans defeated France and occupied Paris in 1940, the German government took over the fashion houses and restricted their sales to only their Axis allies and neutral countries. American and British designers were left to fill the void. New styles featured wide, padded shoulders, narrow waists, and draping over skirts.

In addition to food and gas rationing, in 1942 the United States issued restrictions on the amount of fabric that could be used to make dresses, jackets, trousers, and skirts. This list of do's and don'ts for manufacturers was called "L-85." Day dresses were limited to 3.5 yards of fabric; skirts could be no more than 78 inches around, and the number of buttons, pleats, and pockets also was limited. Trimmings could be no more than 3/8 of a yard, and the height of high heels was fixed at 1.5 inches. Metal zippers were banned, so hooks and eyes and snaps were used instead. Corset manufacturing also was limited, so

This Toledo, Ohio, bride and her bridesmaid wear matching dresses with sweetheart necklines, gathered bodices, and elbow-length sleeves.

47

women were encouraged to go without a girdle. Finally, nylon and silk were needed to make parachutes, so women dealt with the shortage of sheer stockings by using an eyebrow pencil to paint an imitation seam up the backs of their legs to simulate the seam of regular stockings.

The dresses and patterns that fit into L-85 restrictions were called "Utility" dresses. Bodices fit close to the body with a natural waistline and a straight or A-line skirt. Seams and slight gathering in unusual parts of the dress replaced the attached decorations of previous styles. These restrictions had the effect of "freezing" fashion at the 1940 styles.

Maternity and wedding gowns did not have all these restrictions, although the scarcity of materials limited them to rayon satins, crepes, and taffetas in slender styles, with very few decorations. One style of bridal dress that was popular for both brides and bridesmaids had a gathered seam down the center front of the bodice.

The start of World War II resulted in many hurried weddings as couples married either to prevent the groom from being drafted into the service or to wed before the man shipped off to the war. Brides often only had time to get a good dress to wear for their quickie wedding. (Later in the war, being married would not solve the draft issue.)

Although bridal gowns were rarely worn in these quickie weddings, brides often wore embellished dresses. Smocked yokes, gathered bodices,

When women saw movie stars on the screen wearing hats like the ones these actresses are wearing in *Four Jills in a Jeep*, they copied them, even in their bridal headpieces.

narrow belts, and slightly pleated skirts were not uncommon. Bridesmaids often wore dresses with smocking on the bodice for decoration, bows at the neckline, wide belts, and stitched pleat skirts. A small matching straw hat might sport a feather or other decoration to liven it up.

Fashionable two-piece dresses, often with a yoke piece creating the front of the bodice, padded shoulders, and pleated fabric, or dressier suits also were popular, usually paired with an A-line skirt. Hats, gloves, and low-heeled shoes usually were worn by brides and bridesmaids alike. The bridal party often accessorized their otherwise simple dresses with boutonnieres and corsages.

Of course, not all brides were married in quick ceremonies. Some brides did, in fact, have both the time and resources for a more traditional event, complete with gown, veil, and flowers. Typical bridal gowns of the early

This wedding party from May 16, 1942, wears headpieces copied from Hollywood. This bride's dress has a broad satin collar over lace fabric. The bridesmaids all wear similar dresses, but with three different kinds of skirts.

1940s often featured bodices with puffy sleeves that ended below the elbow. Skirts were gathered, reaching just to the floor or with a train. Bridal dresses were often made of satin, crepe, chiffon, or taffeta, while velvet was used for some bridesmaids' dresses. At the beginning of the 1940s, headpieces were often adorned with small flowers on top of her veil.

Hollywood fashions continued to have a big influence on women, and many fashion trends started in the movies. One trend in particular that showed up in bridal fashions in the mid-1940s was the hat. Everyday hats were either small and worn perched on the front of the head or large-brimmed and worn sitting on the back of the head to frame the face. A woman may not have had an exciting dress because of the war restrictions, but there were no restrictions on hats, so they got pretty wild and perked up their wearers.

This young woman was photographed on January 7, 1945, sporting a typical mid-1940s dress with gathered center on the bodice and double-layered peplum over the skirt.

The bridesmaids in this military wedding are wearing large hats in gathered chiffon that match their dresses. The bride's headpiece is starched lace with veiling.

Bridal headpiece fashions were often styled to resemble hats seen in the movies. Both brides and bridesmaids wore hats of straw or fabric, decorated by bows, flowers, or veils. Another popular style featured the headpiece being above the head, often in satin or velvet over a wire frame. Some brides wore headpieces of starched lace and a two-tiered veil.

During World War II, bridal bouquets were made of whatever flowers were available, and roses, chrysanthemums, lilies, Shasta daisies, and even

This bride carries a white gladiola bouquet and wears a sheer dress with rows of lace for decoration. A headpiece of wax flowers on a wire frame features a long, two-tiered veil that covers her large train.

The maid of honor and bridesmaids have sheer lace peplums decorating their plain crepe dress skirts and matching elbow-length fingerless gloves. The bride's satin dress has lace appliqués around the neckline.

This Chicago bride's satin dress has a low neckline filled in by a sheer fabric.

gladiolas were used. As bouquets got smaller, they were made to look larger with lace and net gathered around them. Wide, net ribbons and bouquet waterfalls were added to increase their size, too.

In the mid-1940s fashion styles changed with the addition of peplums, short layers of fabric draped over the skirt. Peplums were draped all around the woman's hips, or shorter in front and longer in back. The peplum fashion trend was featured in bride and bridesmaids styles, often in lace fabric. At the same time, elbow-length fingerless gloves of dress fabric were seen in bridal fashions.

World War II ended with VJ Day on August 15, 1945. Soon after, clothing restrictions were lifted and fashion changes started again. Paris designer Christian Dior's "New Look" fashions featured a decidedly more feminine look that accentuated the bust, with nipped-in waist and fuller, longer skirts, and they influenced fashion in Europe and America. This was a welcome change from the severe military look during the war.

By 1945, there was a change in bridal fashions, too. Bodices became simpler with low necklines filled with sheer fabric for modesty. Wide, flat collars and long sleeves became common, as did appliqués. Satin dresses with sheer fabric-filled bodices, pointed waistlines, long sleeves with puffy tops and close-fitting bottoms, and gathered skirts were typical of postwar gowns. Bridesmaids' dresses often featured bodices with open necklines edged with wide ruffles, gathered center panels, short puffy sleeves,

This wedding party shows the change in wedding fashions after World War II. The bridesmaids are wearing long faux sleeves that match their dresses.

dropped waistlines and gathered skirts drawn up at the bottom and decorated with fabric flowers. Long faux sleeves that matched their dresses also were common.

As GIs returned home after World War II, there was a rush to get married and start families. This resulted in a jump in the birth rate that remained high for the next decade—the "baby boom." These new families needed their own homes, and new suburbs took shape as builders hurried to build small, affordable starter homes for returning veterans.

After World War II, industries began manufacturing consumer goods again. Industry in Britain and Europe had been severely damaged during the war, but American industry did not suffer as much, so it geared up and began providing goods to the rest of the world. This resulted in a period of well-paying jobs and security for American workers that would last through the 1950s.

The bridesmaids in this Moline, Iowa, wedding party are wearing fashionable dresses for 1949. The bridesmaids have double-layer flat collars around their sheer-filled necklines.

FURTHER READING

Baker, Patricia. *Fashions of a Decade: The 1940s*. Facts on File, 1997.

Bond, David. *The Guinness Guide to 20th Century Fashion*. Guinness Publishing Ltd., Enfield, Middlesex, 1988.

Costantino, Maria. *Fashions of a Decade: The 1930s*. Facts on File, 1992.

Editors of Time–Life Books. *This Fabulous Century: 1910–1920*. Time–Life Books, 1969.

Fogg, Marnie. *Vintage Weddings: One Hundred Years of Bridal Fashion and Style*. Lark/Sterling Publishing Co. Inc., 2011.

Kallen, Stuart A., Editor. *The Roaring Twenties*, History Firsthand series. Greenhaven Press, Inc., San Diego, CA, 2002.

Langley, Susan. *Roaring '20s Fashions: Deco*. Schiffer Publishing Ltd., Atglen, PA, 2006.

Nunn, Joan. *Fashion in Costume, 1200–1980*. Schocken Books, New York, 1984.

Press, Petra. *A Cultural History of the United States—Through the Decades: The 1930s*. Lucent Books, Inc., San Diego, CA, 1999.

Uschan, Michael V. *A Cultural History of the United States—Through the Decades: The 1910s*. Lucent Books, Inc., San Diego, CA, 1999.

Uschan, Michael V. *A Cultural History of the United States—Through the Decades: The 1940s*. Lucent Books, Inc., San Diego, CA, 1999.

Walford, Jonathan. *Forties Fashion: From Siren Suits to the New Look*. Thames & Hudson, New York, 2008.

Woog, Adam. *A Cultural History of the United States—Through the Decades: The 1900s*. Lucent Books, Inc., San Diego, CA, 1999.

INDEX